Explore!
FAIR TRADE

Jillian Powell

WAYLAND

Published in paperback in 2014
by Wayland
Copyright © Wayland 2014

Wayland
338 Euston Road
London NW1 3BH

Wayland Australia
Level 17/207 Kent Street
Sydney, NSW 2000

Editors: Victoria Brooker and Julia Adams
Designer: Elaine Wilkinson
Picture Researcher: Shelley Noronha
Illustrations for step-by-steps: Peter Bull

British Library Cataloguing in Publication Data

Fair trade. -- (Explore!)
   1. Competition, Unfair--Juvenile literature.
   I. Series
   338.5'22-dc23

ISBN: 978 0 7502 8335 9

Printed in China

10 9 8 7 6 5 4 3 2 1

Wayland is a division of Hachette Children's
Books, an Hachette UK company
www.hachette.co.uk

Picture acknowledgements:
The author and publisher would like to thank the
following agencies and people for allowing these
pictures to be reproduced:

Cover (top and bottom left, 16) Simon Rawles
(top right) © Joerg Boethling / Alamy
bottom (left) Vetta collection/iStockphoto;
p 2 (right) Bintou Dembele (left and 7 top)
PavelSvoboda/Shutterstock; p4 © Photoshot; p5
(top) Divine Chocolate (bottom) © imagebroker/
Alamy; p6 (top) Swapan/ Shutterstock (bottom)
HYPERLINK "http://www.shutterstock.
com/gallery-503215p1.html" Darrin Henry
Shutterstock; p7 (top) Bintou Dembele (middle)
Rehan Qureshi/Shutterstock (bottom left) Tristan
tan/Shutterstock (bottom right) Maks Narodenko/
Shutterstock; p8 (middle) Shutterstock; p 9 (left)
Alasdair James/iStockphoto (middle) Marcus
Lyons, (right) Lasse Kristensen/Shutterstock; p
10 Jean-Daniel Sudres/Hemis/Corbis; p 11 (top)
Simon Rawles, (bottom) AFP/Getty Images; p12
Amit Dave/X01413/Reuters/Corbis; p 13 (top)
westphalia/iStockphoto
 (bottom) Divine Chocolate; p 14 © Bruce
Coleman/Photoshot; 15 (top) Nigel Cattlin/
Visuals Unlimited/Corbis (bottom) Divine
Chocolate; p 16 Simon Rawles; 17 (top and
bottom) Fair Trade; p18 and p19: Conserve
India; p 20 © MOHSIN RAZA/Reuters/Corbis;
p 21 (top) © Rahat Dar/epa/Corbis; (bottom)
R-O-M-A, Shutterstock; p 22 Divine Chocolate;
p 23 (top) © Ocean/Corbis; p 23 (bottom) Ray
Roberts/Rex Features; p 24 © Simon Kimber/
Demotix/Demotix/Demotix/Corbis; p25 (top)
Marco Secchi/Rex Features (bottom) YURI
CORTEZ/AFP/Getty Images

Contents

Fair trade for all

Fair trade is a way of trading which helps people who farm or make goods in developing countries sell their products at a fair price. Developing countries are countries where many people still work on the land and live on very little money. Fair trade pays them a fair price for their produce so they can earn more and work their way out of poverty.

Machinery helps farmers in developed countries to keep their prices low.

Why is trade not fair?

Farmers in developing countries often find it hard to match the prices for goods that growers from developed countries can offer. In developed countries, farmers can afford to buy machinery that keeps their costs down. They may also be given money grants by governments to help them. In developing countries, farmers can face challenges such as mountainous land or a climate that brings hurricanes or drought. Often they cannot afford to buy machinery or use the latest technology. This makes their costs higher so they cannot match the low prices offered by the farmers in developed countries.

The Fairtrade premium pays for community projects like this water pump at a school in Ghana, West Africa.

The Fairtrade premium

The fair trade system pays a fair price, but it also pays extra money – called the Fairtrade premium – to support community projects such as wells for clean water, schools or health clinics. It encourages safe working practices and farming methods that will help to improve the environment.

Fair trade organisations

The World Fair Trade Organisation (WFTO) was set up in 1989 to make global trading fairer. Members include farmers, growers, producers and traders from all over the world. Another global network, Fairtrade Labelling Organisations (FLO) International, awards the Fairtrade mark to produce that meets international standards for fair trade. There are many smaller fair trade organisations, such as cooperatives, which are groups of farmers working together to provide goods to sell under the Fairtrade mark.

Global market

Thousands of goods are grown or produced by Fairtrade farmers and growers around the world. They include fruit, vegetables, rice, nuts, honey, tea, coffee, sugar, spices, wine, cocoa, flowers, gold, clothing, homewares, beauty products and sports balls.

Sugar cane - Malawi, South Africa

Farmers in the Kasinthula cooperative grow Fairtrade sugar. They have used the Fairtrade premium to pay for clean drinking water and electricity in workers' homes and to fund schools and a community health clinic.

Coffee - Costa Rica

The Coocafé coffee cooperative has over 3,500 farmers producing over 4,000 tonnes of Fairtrade coffee beans each year on small farms. It employs or helps around 15,000 local people. The coffee is grown under the shade of other trees, providing a wildlife habitat and protecting the rainforest.

Tea – Makaibari, India

Fairtrade tea is grown organically without using chemical fertilisers and pesticides. The tea bushes grow on mixed plantations with other plants and forest trees which provide a wildlife habitat. The Fairtrade premium has been used to bring electricity to villages, and fund schools and health clinics.

Cotton – Gujarat, India

The Agrocol Pure and Fair Cotton Grower's Association has nearly 2,000 members, growing 6,000 hectares of organic cotton. Without Fairtrade, cotton pickers worked long hours for little pay and had health problems caused by harmful chemical pesticides.

Cacao – Ghana, West Africa

The Kuapa Kokoo cocoa cooperative represents almost 50,000 cacao growers, growing cacao beans, which are used to make chocolate, on small family farms where cacao grows with other trees.

Bananas – Dominican Republic

The Banelino cooperative has over 340 members. The Fairtrade premium has helped fund schools and medical clinics close to banana farms. It also funds a sports curriculum to tackle problems of drugs and alcohol amongst the young.

History of fair trade

1860s

The novel 'Max Havelaar' by Eduard Douwes Dekker raises the issue of fair trade as the hero fights for better conditions for coffee pickers in Dutch overseas colonies. His name is later used to brand the first fair trade coffee from Mexico.

The cover of the novel 'Max Havelaar'.

1950s

A handmade Chinese pin cushion.

In the US, a shop selling fairly traded craftwork imported from Puerto Rico opens.

In Europe, Oxfam shops begin selling crafts made by Chinese workers living on camps in Hong Kong.

1960s

The United Nations brings the idea of trade rather than charity aid as a means of helping developing countries into its international agreements and actions.

In the Netherlands, the importing organisation Fair Trade Original is set up and the first fair trade 'world shop' opens, selling craftwork.

In Africa, Asia and South America, fair trade organisations are set up to offer advice and support to producers.

The fair trade movement grew up in the mid-20th century, although the ideas that shaped it can be traced at least a hundred years earlier. Today it is global movement with produce traded by farmers, producers, cooperatives, importers and exporters, retailers and support organisations around the world.

1970s	1980s	1990s	2000s

1970s

Traidcraft is founded by Christians in the UK. It combines a trading company with a charity that funds development programmes in developing countries and campaigns for fairer trading.

Fair Trade Original imports the first fair trade coffee from small cooperatives of farmers in Guatemala.

1980s

Some Fairtrade products

The International Fair Trade Association (now the World Fair Trade Organisation – WFTO) is founded as the first global fair trade organisation.

1990s

UK charities work with Traidcraft to set up the Fairtrade Foundation.

Green and Black's launch the first Fairtrade chocolate called Maya Gold.

The Fairtrade Labelling Organisation (FLO) is formed to agree international standards for a Fairtrade mark.

2000s

Garstang in Lancashire, UK, becomes the first 'Fairtrade town' in the world.

FLO introduces the Fairtrade mark for produce.

WFTO introduces the Fair Trade Organisation (FTO) mark for member organisations.

Footballs become the first manufactured Fairtrade products.

By 2011, Fairtrade sales reach nearly US$6 billion worldwide.

Bananas

Bananas are an important part of life for the people of the Windward Islands in the Caribbean. Around half the population rely on income from the banana crop for their living, and bananas make up half of all exports.

The problem with bananas

Bananas are grown on small, family-run farms, but as the price of bananas has fallen worldwide, it is getting harder for farmers to support their families. They can spend more than half their earnings on fertilisers, pesticides, packaging and transport from their farms to the docks. The land is steep and hilly, and the tropical climate can bring damaging hurricanes. Crops can also suffer damage from drought or outbreaks of disease, which can reduce harvests by up to a half.

This woman is washing and packing bananas for export.

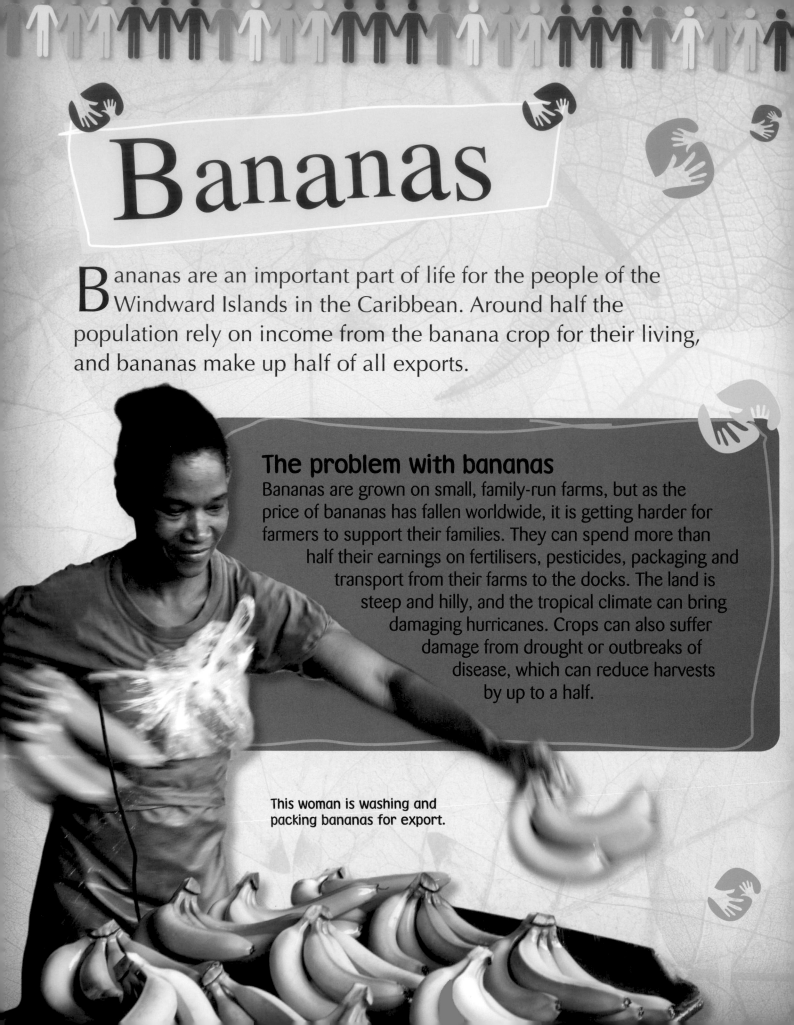

The Fairtrade market

It has become increasingly hard for farmers to compete with the big, international companies that can produce cheap 'dollar bananas' (bananas grown for the US market). These have been grown on large plantations in South America and Africa, which have lower labour costs and make more use of chemical fertilisers and pesticides. Fairtrade helps farmers to compete with these bigger companies. In return for Fairtrade prices and premiums, they agree to use environmentally-friendly practices, such as not using genetically modified (GM) seed, and making sure that plastic used to protect banana trees is recycled or disposed of responsibly.

Community projects

The Fairtrade premium helps to fund community projects on the islands including hospitals and healthcare clinics, clean water supplies, school buses, desks and chairs for primary schools, and improvement to roads and bridges. It helps farmers to improve the quality of their produce, and to buy fertilisers, packaging materials and trucks for transporting crops. It can also help when crops are damaged or destroyed by hurricanes, by funding work to repair damage and replant trees.

Hurricane Dean destroyed crops on the Windward islands in 2007.

Water

Fair trade is not just about people and communities. It is also about improving the local environment. Fair trade organisations work with local communities to tackle problems such as lack of access to clean, safe water.

Dirty water

Over a billion people in developing countries lack access to clean water. In parts of Africa and Asia, women and children can spend up to six hours a day walking to fetch water for their families, allowing them less time for work or schooling. Dirty water causes 80 per cent of diseases in developing countries and over 2 million people, mainly children, die from them each year. As the world's population grows and we need more and more water, the amount available for each person is expected to fall by a third by 2025.

Women often have to walk miles a day to fetch clean water for their families or businesses.

Saving water

Fairtrade works with farmers to save and recycle water. In the western highlands of Kenya, Fairtrade flower farmers protect local water supplies by growing flowers using hydroponics, a method of growing plants without soil, using water containing nutrients. This can use up to 90 per cent less water than growing in soil. They also recycle water for use on other crops, and prevent pollution of water sources from chemical pesticides. Finlay Flowers in Kericho, Kenya, have created wetland areas (areas of lakes and marshes) on their flower farms to recycle and purify water used in their packing houses.

Farming uses 70 per cent of available fresh water.

Funding development

Many Fairtrade farmers and growers working in regions where access to clean water is a problem, use the Fairtrade premium to help pay for digging wells, installing pumps or piping clean water to people's homes and businesses.

A Fairtrade brand of bottled water, 'Ethos', has also been created to help fund water, sanitation and hygiene education programmes. For every bottle sold in the U.S., five cents goes towards development funds.

The Fairtrade premium has helped fund piped water for families living in Ghana.

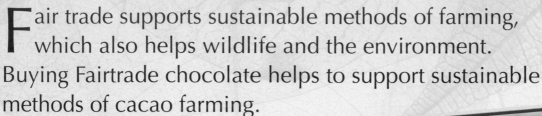

Chocolate

Fair trade supports sustainable methods of farming, which also helps wildlife and the environment. Buying Fairtrade chocolate helps to support sustainable methods of cacao farming.

A cacao plantation in Malaysia.

Growing cacao

Chocolate is made from cacao beans. Traditionally, cacao beans have been grown on small plantations where a variety of trees provide shade and habitat for birds and other wildlife. But many cacao farmers have begun growing cacao trees as a single crop on large plantations in full sun. These trees produce more beans but they also need more water, pesticides and fertilisers to keep them healthy and disease-free.

Mixed plantations

Most Fairtrade chocolate is organic and shade-grown, which means the cacao trees grow under the canopy of taller rainforest trees. Shade-grown cacao trees produce smaller crops but the trees live longer and produce more flavoursome beans. Farmers can receive income from other crops including rubber, Brazil nuts, limes and chillies. There are also many benefits for wildlife and the environment.

Coconut palms shade cacao on this plantation in the Philippines.

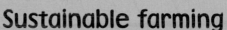

Sustainable farming

Shade trees help to keep the cacao trees healthy. Leaves from shade trees fall to the ground where they break down, returning nutrients to the soil and discouraging weed growth. Soil nutrients fertilise cacao trees and help them resist disease. Shade from surrounding trees help to keep moisture in the soil reducing the need for water. Shade trees also provide a habitat for many species including migratory birds.

Fair trade means fair pay and working conditions on cacao plantations.

Cotton

The Fairtrade cotton market shows how some of the main goals of fair trade work in practice.

Supports small producers
Around 20,000 farmers belong to the Agrocel cotton farmers cooperative in India. Fairtrade means that they can rely on a fair wage and regular work.

A fair price
Fairtrade buyers pay farmers up to 20 per cent more for their cotton crop than they would typically receive on the open market, as it can be sold for a higher price.

Protects traditional skills
Fairtrade cotton is hand picked and spun, and woven on hand looms. Many skills including embroidery, crochet, hand beading and hand block printing are used to design and make cotton clothing, bags and homewares.

Information and communication
There is regular communication and open information all the way through production to sale, from the cotton farmers and workers through to buyers and shoppers.

Good working conditions

Fair working hours and conditions are agreed for workers. Without Fairtrade, cotton pickers had to work long hours for very little pay and had health problems caused by using chemical pesticides.

Equal opportunities/ No child labour

Fairtrade means cotton farms offer equal opportunities regardless of race, caste, religion or gender, and do not employ children, who are used for cheap labour on cotton farms in some countries.

Advertising and promotion

Fashion shows, photography shoots and celebrity support help to raise awareness of Fairtrade cotton and how it improves the lives of cotton farmers.

Development

Growers are offered training and help such as advance payments for orders. Regular orders mean they can plan ahead.

Sustainable farming

Fairtrade cotton is grown organically, without harmful chemical fertilisers and pesticides, using environmentally-friendly methods and dyes. Farmers do not use genetically modified (GM) seed. They use recycled or biodegradable packaging and sea transport rather than air transport, as It produces less carbon emission (CO_2) that contributes to climate change.

Improving lives

The project 'Conserve India' was set up in Delhi to help improve the lives of the poorest people living in the city's slums. The company uses recycled materials to make bags and other goods, that are sold to Fairtrade buyers around the world. Here, an office worker explains how it works.

Q You work for Conserve India. Can you explain what it does and how it helps Fairtrade?

A The project was set up to help recycle the 8,000 tonnes of waste Delhi produces every day. We turn waste plastic bags and other scrap materials into colourful bags, belts, mats and jewellery that we sell mostly to Fairtrade buyers. We have the same values and goals as they do.

Q How much of a problem is plastic waste?

A Plastics are a major environmental problem because most types do not biodegrade in landfills. We take in between 20 to 25 kilograms of plastic bags every day.

Q How does the project help local people?

A Many people locally work as rag pickers, picking up rags and other waste from rubbish piles to sell on for a little money. We pay the rag pickers three times their normal wage to collect waste for us. We also offer them training to give them skills for jobs in shops, offices or factories, or loans to set up new businesses.

Q Who designs your products?

A Our founder, Anita Ahuja, works with a team of designers. Some are design school students or young people on work placements or volunteer programmes.

Q How many people are involved?

A The project currently supports more than 100 rag pickers, and we have over 50 employees.

Q Many of the rag pickers live in slums. How does the project help their families?

A The extra money they earn helps them to build simple homes and feed their families. We also help to fund schools for their children, health clinics and welfare projects.

Q What products does the range include?

A All kinds of handbags, tote bags, beach and evening bags, shoppers, wallets, and belts. They come in every size, shape and colour, but all are made without using any additional chemical dyes.

Q What are the project's future plans?

A We are constantly developing new products, experimenting with different waste materials such as car seat belts, car tyre tubes, denim jeans…the possibilities are endless!

Footballs

In Sialkot, Pakistan, nearly half the population, around 40,000 workers, rely on making footballs for their living. Many of the world's footballs are made here. But in the past, the industry has used low paid piece-workers, including women and children, working long hours in poorly run stitching centres.

An experienced worker can stitch two or three footballs a day.

Work and wages

Fairtrade means that employers must agree to pay workers fair pay, at least the national minimum wage (a minimum amount set by the government) and provide them with secure jobs. On average, wages have increased by around 50 per cent. Fairtrade also prevents children working in factories and provides proper health and safety measures in the workplace. A number of small stitching centres have been set up, near to family homes, making it easier for women to get to work. Employers have to provide good lighting, fresh air and access to drinking water.

Stitching centres

A Fairtrade football can cost little more than one sold under a big brand name, but it can make a real difference to the workers who make it. The footballs are handmade from leather patches that are stamped out and stitched together. One worker can stamp out patches for between 300–400 footballs a day. The patches and the inside casings then go to stitching centres to be sewn together into balls. Experienced workers can stitch two or three footballs a day, which are then sent to the factory to be checked and packed for shipping.

Choosing to play with a Fairtrade football can make a real difference to people's lives.

Development projects

The Fairtrade premium is used to fund community and development projects, including healthcare schemes, and schools for children, which are often run alongside the stitching centres where their parents are working. Fairtrade is also supporting young people in Sialkot by providing small loans to help them start up new businesses such as opening video shops or snooker halls.

Debating fair trade

Fair trade helps to improve the lives of people in developing countries, few would argue against that. But is it enough? Does buying Fairtrade products just make buyers in developed countries feel better, when what is needed is real change in the developing world, in terms of industry and development? What do you think?

For

- It is worth paying a little more for Fairtrade produce because you are helping to improve people's lives.

- Fairtrade helps farmers in developing countries become self-sufficient.

- Farmers and growers can use the Fairtrade premium to improve the efficiency of their businesses and the quality of their produce.

- Fairtrade supports development projects such as schools, health clinics and clean water supplies.

- Buying local produce in developed countries is not always environmentally-friendly. Growing out-of-season fruit and vegetables in heated greenhouses and polytunnels uses fuel and that creates carbon emissions.

The Fairtrade premium helped pay for this new school.

Against

- Fairtrade products are more expensive, and not everyone can afford to buy it. If buyers are on a tight budget, they can't afford to pay the extra.

- Fairtrade makes buyers in developed countries feel good about the choices they make when they shop. But it only provides a few extra dollars a day for the poor. The only thing that will bring lasting change to communities is real progress in industry and development.

- Farmers can come to depend on the Fairtrade premium. What they really need is investment to make their production methods modern and competitive.

- Fairtrade only helps a small number of producers who get the Fairtrade premium. It can encourage farmers to go on growing one crop when prices fall, when they would be better switching to other crops that will sell better.

- Fairtrade produce often has to be transported by air to keep it fresh. This adds to 'food miles', the amount of carbon produced when food is transported. Carbon emissions contribute to climate change, so it makes more sense to buy locally produced food which does not have so far to be transported.

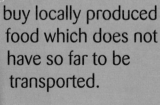

This market in Bristol, UK, encourages people to buy local west country produce.

There are over 1,000 Fairtrade towns across all continents of the world. Cities, towns, boroughs and villages can apply to become Fairtrade towns if they meet five main goals:

1) Councils agree to use Fairtrade products at meetings and events.

2) Fairtrade products are available in shops, cafes and other outlets.

3) Workplaces and organisations buy Fairtrade products wherever possible.

4) Local media raise awareness of Fairtrade.

5) A steering group meets regularly to promote Fairtrade locally.

Fairtrade towns

Raising awareness

Events

World Fair Trade Day is held once a year in May and, around the world, different countries celebrate Fair Trade Month and Fairtrade Fortnight to raise awareness of Fairtrade issues and products. Special events are held, such as tea, chocolate and wine tastings, debates and quiz nights, Fairtrade food markets and recipe promotions.

Schools, universities, churches and mosques can apply to become Fairtrade organisations by providing evidence that they meet key goals.

Communities

Fairtrade schools must:
- Elect steering groups that meet once a term
- Write their own Fairtrade policy or plan
- Use Fairtrade products where possible e.g. tea and coffee, sports balls
- Teach children about Fairtrade in at least three subjects
- Campaign for Fairtrade through school and community events

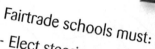

Celebrities

Celebrities help to spread the Fairtrade message by appearing for press launches, fashion shoots or promotions. Chris Martin of Coldplay (middle) gathered signatures for Oxfam's 'Big Noise' petition for fair trade while on tour, and delivered it to the World Trade Organisation summit in Mexico in 2003. Actress Emma Watson has designed clothing collections for People Tree, using organic Fairtrade cotton.

Make it Fairtrade!

Make a yummy fruit ice cream sundae using Fairtrade ingredients. You can adapt the sundae by using different Fairtrade fruits, flavoured ice cream or yoghurt, and milk (or white) chocolate sprinkles, but make sure they all have the Fairtrade mark!

You will need:

Two scoops Fairtrade vanilla ice cream

One Fairtrade mango

One teaspoon Fairtrade clear honey

Small Fairtrade banana

One Fairtrade kiwi fruit

One dessert spoon Fairtrade blueberries

Two squares of dark Fairtrade chocolate

A tall sundae glass

A small grater

Ice cream scoop

Dessert spoons

Vegetable knife

Blender

Mug

1 First prepare your ingredients. They should all have the Fairtrade mark!

Peel and slice the banana. Peel and chop the kiwi into small slices.

2 Peel and chop the mango. Place the pieces in a blender and blend until smooth.

3 Wash and place the blueberries into a mug with the honey.

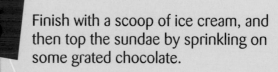

4 Assemble your Fairtrade sundae by spooning a layer of mango purée into the bottom of the glass. Next, alternate a scoop of ice cream with layers of kiwi fruit, honeyed blueberries and sliced banana.

5 Finish with a scoop of ice cream, and then top the sundae by sprinkling on some grated chocolate.

Facts and figures

WFTO has over 450 members worldwide, and operates in 75 countries.

Around 65 per cent of WTFO members are based in Asia, the Middle East, Africa and South America. The rest come from North America, the Pacific Rim and Europe.

The FTO certification mark is awarded to members who meet WFTO standards for fair trading and business practices.

Over 7.5 million people benefit from Fairtrade in more than 60 developing countries.

There are more than 4,500 products that carry the Fairtrade mark, such as food products, wines, beers, cotton, clothing, homewares, gold, beauty products, craftwork and sports balls.

There are over 1,000 Fairtrade towns around the world, on all major continents.

The global market for Fairtrade products reached nearly US$6 billion in 2011, with coffee the biggest seller globally.

Bananas, chocolate and coffee are the top Fairtrade sellers worldwide, with one in four bananas sold in the UK carrying the Fairtrade mark.

More than 560 producer groups supply Fairtrade goods to the UK.

Coffee is the top Fairtrade seller in the USA. Chocolate is the biggest Fairtrade seller in Australia.

Glossary

Biodegradable Decomposes (breaks down) naturally.

Caste A social group of the same rank.

Climate change Gradual warming (or cooling) of world temperatures.

Cooperatives People working together for a shared purpose.

Developing countries Countries where industries need to grow and many people still work on the land and live on very little money.

Drought Long periods with little or no rain.

Exporters Companies who export goods from a country.

Exports Goods sold to foreign countries.

Fair trade A system of trading run by member organisations which helps growers and producers in developing countries sell their produce at a fair price.

Fertiliser A chemical or natural substance (such as manure) used to make a crop more productive.

Genetically modified Where genes (characteristics in cells passed from one generation to the next) have been altered by scientists.

Habitat Natural environment of/for plants and animals.

Importers Companies who import goods to a country.

Migratory Species that migrate, moving from one region or climate to another with the seasons.

Nutrients Substances in food that can provide energy.

Organic/organically Grown using natural methods without using chemicals to fertilise soil or to kill pests.

Pesticides Chemicals used to kill pests on crops.

Piece-workers Workers paid by the amount/piece of work rather than time.

Plantation A large farm of trees or crops.

Pollinate Fertilise with pollen from male parts of a flower.

Producers The people or companies who make/grow goods.

Sanitation ...people or companies who ...

...about getting rid of toilet waste.

Further reading

BOOKS

Fair Trade? (Talking Points) by Adrian Cooper (Stargazer books, 2007)

Fair Trade (Hot Topics) by Jilly Hunt (Raintree, 2012)

Is that Fair? (Fair Trade) by Mary Atkinson (Heinemann Library, 2009)

Making Good Choices about Fair Trade (Green Matters) by Paula Johanson (Rosen Central, 2009)

Websites

www.traidcraft.co.uk
The website for Traidcraft, a charity and campaign organisation, in the UK.

www.fairtrade.org.uk
The website for the Fairtrade Foundation in the UK.

www.fairtrade.org.uk/schools
A website dedicated to Fairtrade schools.

www.wfto.com
The website for the World Fair Trade Organisation.

Index